Rebel Poet

Also by Louis V. Clark III (Two Shoes)

How to Be an Indian in the 21st Century

Rebel Poet

**(Continuing the Oral Tradition)
More Stories from a 21st Century Indian**

LOUIS V. CLARK III

(Two Shoes)

WISCONSIN HISTORICAL SOCIETY PRESS

Published by the Wisconsin Historical Society Press
Publishers since 1855

The Wisconsin Historical Society helps people connect to the past by collecting, preserving, and sharing stories. Founded in 1846, the Society is one of the nation's finest historical institutions.
Join the Wisconsin Historical Society: wisconsinhistory.org/membership

Publication of this book was made possible thanks to the generous support of the Wisconsin Historical Society Readers Circle. For more information and to join, visit support/wisconsinhistory.org/readerscircle.

Printed in Wisconsin, USA
Designed by Percolator Graphic Design

23 22 21 20 19   1 2 3 4 5

Library of Congress Cataloging-in-Publication Data
Names: Clark, Louis V., III, author.
Title: Rebel poet : more stories from a 21st century Indian / Louis V. Clark III (Two Shoes).
Description: [Madison, Wisconsin] : Wisconsin Historical Society Press, [2019]
Identifiers: LCCN 2019009253 (print) | LCCN 2019013279 (ebook) | ISBN 9780870209307 (e-book) | ISBN 9780870209291 | ISBN 9780870209291 (paperback :alk. paper) | ISBN 9780870209307 (e-book)
Subjects: LCSH: Clark, Louis V., III. | Clark, Louis V., III—Poetry. | Oneida Indians—Wisconsin—Biography. | Oneida Indians—Poetry. | Indians of North America—Wisconsin—Biography.
Classification: LCC PS3603.L36526 (e-book) | LCC PS3603.L36526 Z46 2019 (print) | DDC 811/.6 [B]—dc23
LC record available at https://lccn.loc.gov/2019009253

♾ The paper used in this publication meets the minimum requirements of the American National Standard for Information Sciences—Permanence of Paper for Printed Library Materials, ANSI Z39.48-1992.

To my wife, Debbie
Thank you for dancing
Across the rainbowed path
Of my dreams, my hopes
My wishes
To our destiny
Amongst the stars

Contents

Kanuhwelatuksla

Traditional Oneida Thanksgiving Prayer

Now listen to the words that come before all else.

We bring together our minds and give thanks to one another.
So be it our minds.

We bring together our minds and give thanks to our Mother
the Earth, for the life she gives.
So be it our minds.

We bring together our minds and give thanks for the first fruits
that grow, the strawberry.
So be it our minds.

We bring together our minds and give thanks for all the
medicines.
So be it our minds.

We bring together our minds and give thanks to the tobacco
we use to send our messages to the Creator.
So be it our minds.

We bring together our minds and give thanks to all the different
animals that help sustain our lives.
So be it our minds.

We bring together our minds and give thanks to all the different
trees, the maple is the most special of all.
So be it our minds.

We bring together our minds and give thanks to all the waters
great and small.
So be it our minds.

We bring together our minds and give thanks to all the different
birds that entertain us.
So be it our minds.

We bring together our minds and give thanks to the forces that
work together with the earth, our Grandfathers the Thunders,
who bring the rain to renew the earth.
So be it our minds.

We bring together our minds and give thanks to the eldest Brother
the Sun, who gives us light and warmth.
So be it our minds.

We bring together our minds and give thanks to our Grandmother
the Moon, she controls all the life cycles on earth.
So be it our minds.

We bring together our minds and give thanks to the stars that are
our relatives, they beautify the sky.
So be it our minds.

We bring together our minds and give thanks to the four messengers
who give us guidance.
So be it our minds.

We bring together our minds and give thanks to the Creator of all,
for it is the Creator who has brought us together as one.
So be it our minds.

I.

Hello, or, more appropriately, *Segoli!*

My name is Louis V. Clark III.

I am a storyteller.

I am a poet.

I come from two great peoples.

My Father's People came from Poland.

My Mother's People were the Haudenosaunee, The People of the Longhouse.

In 1834, more than seven hundred of my relations left New York on foot.

They journeyed more than one thousand miles to Green Bay, Wisconsin.

My Father's People traveled even farther seeking freedom.

I live in two worlds—not by choice.

I was born and raised on the Oneida reservation of Wisconsin.

I am a member of the Oneida Nation, the People of the Standing Stone.

I was given stories as a child.

And, I've discovered,

Not without a fight,

That stories become foundations.

I've also learned

Negatives in life,

If worn with honor,

Can be something worth having.

Giving us wisdom and strength.

They call me

Two Shoes.

II.

When I was born, Indians were disappearing. It was like the whole world was a giant magician, and they put a piece of cloth over the United States and said, *Abricka Dabricka*, and poof! Now you see us, and now you don't. Television was the new thing, and cowboy shows ruled the airwaves, and no one wanted to be an Indian.

My parents were both hunters. When Dad returned from his stint in Korea (in the Navy), he requested that Mom become his hunting partner. Deer hunting, small game, and even nighttime raids on spawning fish and maybe migrating geese—depending on the emptiness of the freezer. My Gramma—Mom's Mom—told my Mother that if your husband wants to spend time with you, then you spend time with your husband.

Dad loved the cowboy shows, John Wayne, and any movie about World War II. We had a .30-30 rifle similar to the gun used by Lucas McCain in the TV show *The Rifleman*. Dad loved that show; it was about a man and his son and his gun. Dad would get out his .30-30 and demonstrate how he could cock the firing mechanism just like they did on TV. (Years later I, too, mastered this technique.) So I was destined to be a hunter. Around 1960, at about four or five years old, I received a plastic toy .30-30 rifle that shot a spring-loaded bullet. I don't think the rifle lasted me until noon on Christmas day; however, I did show just how good my aim was.

1961 Lucas McCain's Son

I'll never forget
the tiny gold stars
Dad flung over
the Christmas tree branches
how they streamed to the floor
making the carpet glisten.

I'll never forget
that beautiful mess
open boxes
strewn about
packing tissue exploding
like lava pumping
from volcanoes of joy
and I
too young for midnight mass
five years old
with teenaged sisters
sentenced to "be quiet"
as the house slept
I cradled
my new .30-30 Mattel Winchester
plastic-carved trophy
with Chuck Connors's handle
a "chip off the old block"
groomed to hunt
groomed to stalk
french fries, candy, sisters.

Hidden inside
tree branch camo
Mother came down the steps
(discretion the better part of valor)
Christmas dinner noises
called out to Dad
he too
passed through
the danger zone

My oldest sister
who bought donuts
on Saturday mornings
earned her safety
The quarry, younger sister
eight years my senior
who watched American Bandstand
Denied me M-i-c-k-e-y Mouse
came down rubbing her eyes
aim, trigger, hammer
MOTHER!!!
.30-30 rifle gone.
Lectures, punishment
Did Dad smile
at his son's accuracy?

Stories were very important in our town. Television was a passing fancy or something to babysit the children. Radio was for lunchtime breaks with Paul Harvey, dinner breaks with Howard Cosell, or a time for teenage girls to dream away their hours, calling Johnny Sax the Disc Jockey and dreaming of their soldier boys so far away. But the stories people shared at the dinner table, at the tavern, or while stopping at someone's house to visit over a six-pack—these were the stories that set the foundation of life.

When we moved into the heart of the reservation, I was admonished to be nice to the Indians. So I sat outside by the road and asked people passing by if they were Indians—I couldn't tell by looking at them, since they all looked like people to me. If they were to tell me they were Indian, I was going to be nice to them. (I caught h—— for that.) No one ever told me that *I* was an Indian.

One thing I loved immediately about reservation life was going up to the store. The stores were on the same side of the street as our house, so I was free to wander as I pleased to spend my allowance—five cents on Wednesdays and ten cents on Saturdays, when my parents remembered. There were two stores in town, one of which also housed the post office and had a set of steps for sitting and talking. There was always an old man sitting there, willing to tell us stories. I wish I remembered those stories. Perhaps they were magical stories about how the Oneidas came to Wisconsin. Someone claiming to be the Lost Dauphin of France, Eleazer Williams, is said to have led our people to this area. In De Pere there is a place called Lost Dauphin State Park.

Maybe the old man's stories were about how great the Oneida men were at baseball. Summer Sundays would find men in their white short-sleeve shirts, black pants, and shiny black shoes and women in their cotton dresses, all perched on the hoods of their cars surrounding the ball diamonds in the area. When someone hit a home run, the car horns would blare.

Mom told the story of how my Grandpa Jonas and his brother played on an Indian traveling team around 1912 and were picked up by the St. Louis Browns to play a couple of games. I never did the research to see if the story was true; I'd rather just believe it was true because it was a good story. Mom said she played baseball during World War II, though she didn't tell many stories because she was always busy.

Dad liked to make things with his hands. Some Sunday afternoons we would go hunting for white ash branches. This was the best kind of wood for making slingshots. We'd look for the perfect, crutch-shaped piece, and he would skin the bark off and tie the ends to form a slingshot and then would bake the wood in the oven. With this done, he would find a red rubber inner tube and cut out two pieces, each about one inch wide and sixteen inches long. He attached one end of the rubber to a leather patch cut from an old work boot he had saved; this was the stone holder. The other end of the rubber was attached to the white ash crutch. He used special string and had a special way of tying the rubber to each end. It was a work of art.

Dad was a master magician when it came to ropes, knots, and braiding. He said he was trapped in Russia for almost a year during World War II and had plenty of time to study things when he wasn't busy collecting cigarette butts, taking out the leftover tobacco, mixing it with dried horse manure, and selling it on the black market so he had money to travel around the country. One day Dad took a piece of string and wove it through a big button and placed it across both his middle fingers and exercised them back and forth. This made the button spin and made a sound like *voot-voot, voot, voot*. So we called it a voot-voot.

The old storyteller at the store took a piece of string, drilled a hole in the cap of a detergent bottle, inserted one end of the string through the hole and knotted both ends, then placed the cap back on the bottle. He would walk up to someone and squeeze the bottle, causing the string to dance out and tickle the other person's nose. Someone pushed him one night when he did this in the tavern, and he broke his back. Forever after he was on crutches. My Dad didn't have any use for the man who had pushed him, and as history has it Dad beat him up once when they were much younger. Stories.

III.

It was a rude awakening going off to school. Especially where I stood within the family.

Ooops!

Some babies are born
Out of season
Out of time
Shocking their parents
Like I shocked mine.

I don't really think that mine was a planned Catholic pregnancy, one where you are planning on procreation.

I was left to myself most of the time. I had a doll, one arm missing and one eye gone, but it was mine. I had a dog who was more of a hindrance to my exploring than a companion bent on getting into the same type of trouble. The dog's name was Cookie, and she never let me wander too close to danger. She was my babysitter.

I'm sure the teachers didn't mean to burden their one "colored" student. I was taught that Columbus came to this country to save the heathen savages, which was fine until the day I learned the heathen savages were me. First the shocking news that I was an Indian and then the truths revealed on the playground that I was a "stupid Indian" or a "stupid Polack."

My Mom always told me I was special and that I had to treat those kids as special because they weren't as special as me. (This did confuse me just a bit.) My Dad taught me about World War II and the Nazis and Hitler's "Final Solution." I was supposed to be big and strong and willing to fight for what was right. But it is hard and scary when you think you know what is right but nobody seems to want to stand by your side. If you ain't tough enough, you end up getting hurt.

I wrote this poem:

What about God

Just a little bit of quiet
In a world made of noise
No one would even notice
Boys just being boys
There's always someone different
At least or so it seems
The first thing that they take from you
Is your spirit, then your dreams.

It starts as just a whisper
A snicker or a groan
That finds you
In a crowded space
Feeling all alone
The unrepentant comment
That leaves you just confused
Is this really happening?
Am I being abused?

Inside you feel a pain
Nowhere for you to turn
Afraid to stand up for yourself
Afraid that you'll get burned
One bad apple in the bowl
Can spoil the whole bunch
And if you're looking different
You're sure to take a punch.

No one cares to believe you
You think that it's quite odd
That people can be so hurtful
And still believe in God
You take in all their actions
Their will that's known as free
You question their belief in God
But does God believe in me?

I did spend a lot of time thinking. My Dad always had the World
War II stories about the concentration camps and the evil that
happened around the world. As a child, I was told over and over
and over again that to be a good Christian, I would have to humble
myself. All the Saints humbled themselves. I didn't understand.
I always heard of people finding Jesus as though Jesus was lost.
I couldn't understand being led to slaughter without putting up
a fight, so I wrote this poem explaining just how I believed at
the time.

Third-Grade Religion

I guess I'm not the brightest candle
Burning in the church
My flame is bouncing all around
I stumble in my search

Many things I don't understand
Though all things have a cost
Then to find that my Lord Jesus
Would infer that he was lost?

Then to suffer, what does it mean?
Is pain a prerequisite
To enter heaven on my knees
And at his right hand sit

I'm perplexed when given thought
On how I must be humbled
I'm a man, on feet I'll stand
In third grade this I mumbled.

I guess I had an arrogance about me. I'd stand up tall and get knocked down, over and over again. Someone said of me, "he always thinks he's right," and I couldn't argue with that. I knew I was often wrong, but whenever I attempted something, said something, or did something, by gosh, I did always think I was right.

Then I got older and inherited a black walnut tree.

When autumn comes, my black walnut tree releases the fruits of its labors, again and again, over and over, for weeks, or so it seems. One day I picked up and counted twelve hundred black walnuts, which leads to the question, "What type of idiot would count all those black walnuts?" I get everything picked up and— *splosh*—more hit the ground. I hear God in that beautiful old black walnut tree. He has a sense of humor as I realize I am not in control. Yes, I could cut down the tree, but then I'd lose something beautiful. So, I humbly pick black walnuts day after day, knowing that He gave me this tree as a metaphor for life, showing me that I can only do what I can do. I don't have control in this life. (Still, I'll always attempt to stand up for what is right.)

(I added these words to the poem "What about God.")

Can I stand tall against this wind?
Can I on my journey stay?
A humble soul to right some wrongs
For this,
On knee,
I pray!

As a human being I knew I was supposed to stand for something. I probably did a lot of stupid things, said things that I shouldn't have, got into fights that I shouldn't have, and probably hurt people when I should have known better. I wrote this poem, "Playground Bully," about a certain individual who, for a time, enjoyed using my head as a trampoline. Someone would grab me from behind and hold me down while this individual jumped up and down with his knee on my head. (This may explain a lot about my thought process, which I consider a great sense of humor.) I just hope and pray that, in my never-ending fight to fit in, I never become that bully. I know I have crossed boundaries now and then, but I owe a debt of gratitude to the bullies who beat me because they made me see what I never wanted to become.

Playground Bully

My mind whispered secrets
Late at night—under covers
That hid the day's harvest of bruises
Whispered softly, so no one could hear
"He's not so tough"
I know, I know, I know
I know I know.

My salt-tasting lips
Washed with another night's tears
Sang the mantra
To the gods of fear
Each night
Alone
In bed.

I know his secrets
I know his weakness
His size, his parents, something
Made him different
As my skin made me.
I felt sorry for him
Through hair-clenched fists
I beat him each night
He beat me each day
Then
Our union collapsed
A guardian angel hit him
And I wasn't worth
The price any longer
I don't miss him
But
I'll never forget him!

Then there was the confusion of home. There was so much that I didn't understand. My oldest sister became pregnant and fled. My other sister—whom I always called my "youngest sister" even though she was eight years my senior—hid within herself. I just hid.

Growing Up

I was never afraid of the dark
I was afraid to leave them alone
My parents.
They thought that I was afraid
Of the dark
To be alone
The bogeyman

Darkness of the world
Never frightened me
If I couldn't see
Who could see me
I yearned to be the dove
A referee I became

Momma woke Daddy
with a whip
For what he'd done
I don't know
I wasn't afraid
Of the dark
I was afraid
To sleep.

We lived on a roller coaster. We had great highs, and we had "snake belly in wagon rut" lows.

If there was no yelling or screaming in the house, it was a good day. You just retreated inside yourself and tried to find happiness when you could. I had a great imagination. I dreamed of things that I could be. A painter, a gas station attendant, a cowboy (go figure). I thought that I was Superman but somehow I had lost my superpowers. I also wanted to be a football player.

When I was still a little kid, Mom and Dad had a party, and a bunch of teenagers were there. They played tackle football, and I was the only young person who was allowed to play. I got the living daylights kicked out of me, but on a crossing route by the receiver, as I was running with my left arm toward the quarterback, the receiver came by me running the other way. The pass was thrown behind me, but I twisted around and deflected the ball with my left hand. I don't know if I broke anything, but for weeks my ring finger, middle finger, and pointer finger were so swollen that I couldn't close my fist. I hid this from my Mom because she would have taken me to the doctor, where I'd get a penicillin shot and be sent home. (I got so many penicillin shots that I shouldn't ever be sick. Right in the hip, and one time I even bled onto the car seat.) I was always—and I wore this as a badge of honor—asked to play football with the older kids.

Some Sunday evenings I would stagger home, moaning and groaning about how much I hurt. Youth always allowed me to recuperate during the night. I would write stories about the football games and read them to myself as if they were in the newspaper. After all, I was actually Superman, so in my secret identity I had to write newspaper stories. I wrote this poem about the bumps and bruises I encountered growing up and my Father's response to them.

(I realize I'm breaking the flow of the story and poems here, but I'm doing so intentionally because that is what it is like growing up in an alcoholic family. You can't count on anything, but then again, every once in a while, smiles do appear.)

A Poem

And so it goes
A long time ago
I fell
Or so my sister said
(though I was pushed
Rings in my head)
From the car
Into the snow.

I broke my leg before I could walk
I broke my nose before I could talk
Seems
My guardian angel was
An accident waiting to happen.

I knew no fear
(nor common sense)
Strong, stubborn, willful
Never shedding a tear
To wash away stupidity
I climbed to the sky
With Momma's fitted sheet
To prove I could fly.

My sisters both screamed
My sisters both cackled
Before I could jump
I was ingloriously tackled
I adopted the motto
In God I trust

I'd rather wear out
Than sit here and rust.

My Daddy shook his head
Said someday you'll pay
For all this foolishness
You commit today
I looked at my Dad
With a beer in his hand
I rose up tall
I took a stand
My motto is this
In God I trust
I'd rather wear out
Than sit here and rust.

So I broke in horses
They broke me too
Got hit by a car
Turned black and blue
Wrestled in high school
College and coached
Worked in the sun
Until I was poached

Jumped off a cliff
Why? I don't know
To prove I'm a man
The seeds that I'd sow
Played tackle football
No pads feeling sporty

Separated my shoulder
Playing football at forty

Past fifty played baseball
Stole second base
To be honest a wild pitch
If you ask
Just in case
But I've stood by my motto
In God I trust
I'd rather wear out
Than sit here and rust.

Though now in my years
My wisdom abounds
Paid too much attention
To fools and to clowns
My Daddy was right
Though God I still trust
It may have been less painful
To sit here and rust!

The dining room table held a special place of honor in most houses
during the 1960s. People would gather, play cards, talk, argue, and
in our house drink beer. I did a lot of listening to some crazy sto-
ries. Like the time someone showed up in the middle of the night.
The car ahead of them had hit a deer. There was no real damage to
the car, so our friends said they'd call the authorities and take care
of the deer. Instead they threw the deer into the trunk of their 1965
Mustang and drove into our garage. When Dad opened the trunk,
the deer jumped out. Barbaric as it may have been, we had venison
for dinner soon after. This was a much-repeated story.

Then the Beatles came to the States, and hair became a much talked about subject. It was interesting that all the boys I knew on the reservation had very short hair, while all the city kids had long hair. I also noticed that most of the men we knew from off the reservation had an overabundance of body hair. I didn't have any body hair (sixty years later I basically still don't), and neither did anybody else I saw working on the reservation. My cousins, big, strong men who did concrete work, often had their shirts off—no hair there. I think it was a survival mechanism, in the evolutionary sense. People in the old days would shoot at us. They shot animals, they shot Indians, so it is no wonder that Indians and animals are mascots.

I wrote this poem:

Whew!

I don't know: did Injuns scalp?
Or is it just a story?
Made up for the press you know
To give the Cowboys glory
Indians are different than white men
White men are covered in fur
I'm glad that I'm an Indian
For this reason I am sure
All the troubles I have seen
All the storms that I have weathered
I'm afraid they'd shoot me for the fur
'Stead of shooting me for my feathers.

Little boys don't understand grown-up rules and problems. Maybe I'm still a little boy, because I still don't understand.

1960s

His and hers Kimonos
A muumuu for my Mom
Nixon wants the White House
Khrushchev has the bomb
Dino's drinking every night
Singing words of love
Crouching low beneath my desk
Are bombs falling from above?

Tasting crackers that had no taste
Race riots in the South
Headed to Chicago on an oleo run
Daddy said shut your mouth
The fool he won't notice
The smart man he won't say
Friday night piano lessons
"My Bonnie" rolled away

Gin inside the goblets
Whiskey in the den
Momma tasted brandy
A nightmare now and then
Everything's laughs and giggles
It was all for fun
No one was supposed to be hurt
Till we came undone

Sometimes the sound of a little slap
Echoes through the years
Haunting generations

Wrapped in bitter tears
The gossip of a Christian Lady
Who didn't know love at all
Made spectral shadows in my life
And happiness I can't recall.

There were all types of ugly greenish brown containers tucked away in the church basement. Inside was the food we would need to survive if the "Red Army" ever dropped "the bomb" on us. See, it didn't pay to be Red during the 1960s, so no wonder I got beat up all the time.

When my oldest sister received her driver's license, an older woman called and told our Mother that our car was seen going around a curve on two wheels. All hell broke loose when my sister asked, "Who are you going to believe, your own daughter or some old biddy?" I jumped up between my sister and Mother and was thrown to the ground, actually spinning my way across the kitchen floor. My other sister grabbed me and we ran, held each other, and cried. We heard a loud *slap*, and the next morning I found one of the kitchen chairs broken in the basement. Alcohol haunts for years and years as that slapping sound echoes through my life. I can hear it today more than fifty years later.

But life goes on.

Friday night, pre–Vatican II, it seems all good Catholic families are at the tavern eating perch. Sunday morning after mass, a lot of the families walk across the road to the bar. There are a lot of bars between church, St. John the Baptist, and home on a pre–Vatican II Sunday afternoon. Some families can't afford babysitters, and the tavern is the town meeting place.

Three Little Indians

One little two little three little Indians
Friday night they're out in the street again
Mom and Dad just have to have a drink again
Three Little Indian Boys

Just like Catholics eating all the perch again
Potato chips for three little Indians
A candy bar to split 'tween the three of them
Three Little Indian Boys

One little two little three little Indians
Fast asleep while Daddy's driving drunk again
Grim statistics blame it on his race again
Three Little Indian Boys

Three Little Two Little One Little Indian
Soon there'll be just none little Indians
'Cept for mascots dressed like an Indian
Where are the Indian boys?
Where are the Indian boys?

I don't know why we always stopped at the tavern. We would either work or go to the tavern, except during hunting season when we'd hunt and then go to the tavern. I remember "don't tell Mom" and my feelings of guilt as she would take me into the basement with tears in her eyes, like a bare light bulb in the local police station, and question me until I broke down like the coward that I was. I was not a good accomplice. The tavern was a terrible place where the words "just one more" hung across my shoulders like a cross.

Just One More

Little boy lost
In a crowded room
Standing by the door
Laughter rings
Someone shouts
Who wants
"Just one more"?

So it begins
The curse of time
Taverns are the whore
Shadows fall
Haunting men
I mean it
"Just one more."

Candy bars
Potato chips
Shooting pool
And keeping score
The broken word
The broken trust
I promise,
"Just one more...."

If he could swear
If he could scream
Standing silent by the door
For little boys
Statistics show

Sadly he's
Just one more!

It was paradoxical. I was afraid every time my parents went out together because I never knew what type of fight they would bring home. Yet, when they were gone, the house was so peaceful. I wrote this poem to my parents.

Legitimate

Your merging gave me life
But never "a life"
To run to like a savior
Standing with arms outstretched
Ready to take me in
But I run, I run, I run
From the devil's garden
Where physical enjoyment
Physical escape
Blooms upon every tree
Bursting forth like islands
Formed from molten rock
Through receding waters
I run.
Deserts block my way
I pray to quench my thirst
A trickle of love
To flow between
The two of you
So I am not a bastard
Born out of physical passions

Relief without protection
Don't love me
Love each other.

Our house had a stair railing made of dowels like a prison's set of bars. I remember sitting there with my face wedged between the dowels like a convict; but no, I was guarding the steps, the way to my Mother, who was upstairs crying.

Just a Memory

Pulling guard duty
Sitting on the steps
Elbows on knees
Face between the bars
Watching
A sleeping giant's chest
Rising and falling
Rising and falling
A ship on a roller coaster sea

Behind me echoes of sobbing
Today, yesterday, tomorrow
Like a faucet dripping
Dripping, dripping
Somewhere in the distance

Through this shroud of silence
Catlike Mother appeared
The arms meant for comfort
Now point, aim
An imaginary gun

(or signs of the future)
"Pow!" she whispers
"My problems would be over
So easily."

Comes the night
Blankets tucked tight
Around my neck
Like a noose
I face the wall
Like the monkeys
Hear, see, and speak
In case
I become a problem.

I was afraid of what my Mother could do. I slept in the crack
between my bed and the wall, with my pillow bunched up in the
middle of the bed, covered. If I should be shot, it would be the
pillow that took the bullet. Me, I'd slide to the floor, push myself
off the wall, and fly out of the room, down the stairs, and out into
the woods. No one would find me in the dark, in the woods. I did
not sleep until I heard my parents sleeping.

I did know there were better ways to live, so I wrote this poem.

I Choose to Believe in Santa Still

I came to not like holidays
To not like them at all
Holidays meant parties
The calm before the fall
Happy smiles, kisses, hugs

Alcohol and beer
Why the heck have parties
That always end in tears

Learning came on early
Silence in the house
Little boys learned to hide
Quiet as a mouse
But in an early intellect
There was a sacred day
The birth of our dear Jesus
When Santa came to play

I still believe in Santa
Though graying in my hair
I still believe in Santa
The dream is always there
Though broken in my youth
The world called Santa bunk
But Momma said that Santa came
"Here's the keys
Your gift is in the trunk."

I was fast approaching the age where a Jewish boy becomes a man.
I had already fought with the white doctors in the hospital and
lost, so I came up with this poem for this age.

Sorry, Mr. Poe/Lost Tribe of Israel

Once within a sweat lodge dreary
As I pondered naked and weary
About the man Columbus who sailed the sea

It seemed my fate somewhere, somehow
While set inside this great Pow Wow
That everyone just stared and looked at me

Now my skin so nice and tan
My hair so long a feathered band
Born off the rez in hospitals compromised
What could I do?
Not Christian or Jew
Oh, the Doctor's knife—circumcised.

Now I sit all naked and bare
Forced to endure the old one's stare
Making me feel different and quite foolish.
Then a thought in retrospect
I should have said but I neglect
Hey, I'm not white, I'm-I'm-I'm-
Yes! I'm Souixish!

The world really was changing around 1968. I started to live out-
side of myself. I was one person at home, and I was free when
I wasn't at home. I began to spend more and more time in the
woods. I didn't want to deal with the world as it was at home, so
when I was home I really wasn't—just the physical me was there.

Doing Time

Lost inside the reservation
Circa 1968
Crying out for freedom
Society showed us hate

Supporting unions in Memphis
They cut old Martin down
Another gun in old L.A.
Brought Bobby to the ground

Blood continued spilling
Newscasts every night
Moguls on their mountains
Said everything's alright

Put Nixon in the White House
A puppet on a string
Placate a generation
Morals lost their sting

Where is honor granted
When heroes lose their shine
Don't consider what we are
We're only doing time!

Things became weirder and weirder at the house. Maybe it is the natural progression of alcoholism. There were lies and lies upon lies. We catered to the lies. Mom's sick again. Keepsakes and piggy banks disappeared. Bank accounts were closed, and charge accounts were opened and closed at the top of the lungs. Mom looked to suicide. Crying, I begged her to reconsider. How many times? I was always afraid to walk into the house after school, never knowing what I would find. I learned to wash clothes, fold clothes, cook meals, and I guess I learned to lie by keeping silent. There were things wrong, but "you did what you could."

One summer Sunday, yelling again, suicide threat, I called the police. There is still a place inside of my being that agonizes over that decision. Was I right? Was I wrong? Or was I a selfish little boy not wanting to put up with it any longer?

I lost my Grandmother that day; she disowned me for calling the police on my Mother. The family shame, in my heart, was more important than my Mother's life, or so I felt about my Grandmother's conviction. I was told that I wasn't a good son, and maybe I attempted to live up to that condemnation. I fell more and more into myself.

They Made Me Judge

I called them to help me escape
From between two pillars crumbling
My hair growing wild and free
I pushed and pleaded them apart
Till someone vowed to die
On a promise of better days

Containers of milk
Bleeding on the floor
Vicious blows against the wall
She flew past running
To and from the darkest angel
He followed from mixed emotions

Screaming in the orchard
Apple blossoms hiding
From scenes blotting out the sun
His arms wrapped about her
In silence it could have been love
Pulling them to the ground

Guns upon their hips
White coats miles behind
Pulled me apart and away
But I didn't see
Only with my eyes

She never died that day
Alone
We lost her
Anyway.

It was a dark and stormy night. Yes, it was—really. There was a noise, perhaps a scream, the type of scream that pulls you questioning from your sleep. In this state of living, you begin to question everything. Perhaps this is the reason why I attempted so many crazy stunts. The exhilaration of successfully jumping from a high post to another object, or jumping from a ledge into the water and surviving, made me feel like I was actually alive. Yet the failures, and the physical pain encountered, proved more concretely that I was alive. A sick part of me must have found solace in the chance of physical pain, for while the physical pain was manifest, the emotional pain would hide. Sadly, the emotional pain would eventually triumph.

Twelve-Year-Old Boys

Twelve-year-old boys
Twelve-year-old boys
Brings a smile to your face
If you ever were
Or hope to be
A twelve-year-old boy

Twelve-year-old boys
Aloft in their dreams
Invulnerable, immortal, and then
Once upon a midnight scream
Twelve-year-old boys
Awaken into men

Dreams shattered
Innocence scattered
Mother battered
Another piece of the pie
For twelve-year-old boys
Twelve-year-old boys
When innocence dies.

Then I heard the scream again. (Forty-plus years later I still hear the scream.)

Silent Night

A shallow cry
Heard over and again
Like an echo
From
The fallen house of Usher
A protector's cry
One never written
In the lines of heroic novels
But heard in unwritten lives

I retreat inside my covers
Like a turtle inside his shell
I feel the cold gray hand

Of fear clutch my throat
Like a master clutching his whip
To kill all freedom dreams

Then the silence
That holds you like a cell door
Standing like a warrior
Who stands when beaten
Wanting to die proud

I explode into their sacred sanctuary
And see what no child should ever see
Their human-ness
Bleeding on the floor
Swelling like bruises
Upon her face
He slinks away
In shame
She covers herself
The same
And I
I am left alone.

What do you say? What do you do?
The sun comes up.
You eat breakfast.

Reality

Lord, I don't want to be a warrior
I dread the thought of pain
My silence is mistaken for bravery

Like teardrops in the rain
No one can see the thunder
No one can feel the night
I never wanted to be a warrior
I was always forced to fight.

So I read, I sang (when no one was around), and I wrote. I wrote poems, I wrote stories, and I started to smoke; it gave me something to do. I became a prison guard sitting at the bottom of the steps each night, sometimes smoking Dad's cigarettes, waiting to hear snoring. Then it was safe to go to bed.

Waiting

Rituals of torture
Played each night
Dancing in the stairwell
Twitching like a condemned man
Waiting to hear
The click, the latch, the trap door
Sucking life slowly away

Shackled to the step
A galley slave
On a doomed vessel
Bound by guttural sounds
Whispered words of love
Creaking springs
Banging headboards
Counting cigarette butts
And empty beer bottles
On the kitchen counter

Then silence
Silence like the sun
Touching the clouds
Calling day to life
Rhythmic breathing
Snoring from above
And a prayer offered up
To hold on
One more day.

I learned to focus on the moment. I turned away from my roots. I wasn't Indian. I wasn't white. I just was. Oh yes, I heard bad stories about things I was said to have done. But I didn't listen to them. I spent my free time in the barn playing basketball, and in the fall I stayed in the woods. I still had my dreams, but they were just to see me through one more day peacefully. Even getting beaten up at school was okay, as long as there was no fighting at home.

Then my sister got sick, with brain cancer, and I learned how to pray selfishly. First it was to save her life. It was saved, but she still had convulsions and so I became a babysitter. If she convulsed, I was to get a spoon in her mouth to keep her from choking. I prayed long and hard that she would never have a convulsion while I was there. It was a shameful prayer, a shame I carry to this day. I guess I only cared about me.

We did have good times, though, she and I. Just not enough of them. I spent two months watching her fade away in a hospital bed. She died at twenty-one years of age.

The funny thing about my sister passing away was that all of a sudden I was popular. Oh, not with my peers, but with the adults who wouldn't allow me to do what I normally did, which was to go hunting all by myself. They must have thought I was going to shoot myself, but that wasn't going to happen. If I was going to die, it would be from doing something stupid like thinking I could dive off a high dive after never having been on one before. I raced out onto the board, jumped off, and was propelled high into the air, before I landed flat on my back on the water. The water felt like concrete, and then—sans my suit, which had slid down to my knees—I sank to the bottom.

Lessons

I lost my freedom on the high dive
As I flew through the air one day
Twisting and rolling, spinning and turning
Like the angels out to play

My innocence was shattered
My ego was battered
My body was splattered
As I sank like a stone

My suit came undone
My body was numb
My actions were dumb
As I met Davy Jones

Mr. Jones, said I, and held out my hand
As he stared at me with a grin
You thought you were cool, silly old fool
But if you don't try you can't win.

At least my Dad had a sense of humor.

Fathers

The worst thing in life
Is to marry a wife
Who's allergic to bodily odor
They can't understand
That being a man
Isn't all their mommas have told her
Girls see a knight
All shiny and white
Thinking their man is a ringer
Then things become sad
When knights become dads
They all go, "Hey kid, pull my finger!"

And I watched him become a Grand Dad.

What have I become
He said slightly glum
As grandchildren invade his house
He staggers 'round
Like a half-drunk clown
Attempting to be quiet as a mouse

When they're finally asleep
And he tries to keep
His sanity going room to room
Flipping off lights
That burn day and night
Electric bills shoot to the moon

All faucets are dripping
He's always tripping
On wet towels strewn on the floor
And set in concrete
Each toilet seat
Stands upright oh lord what a chore

To put the seat down
He'd say pound for pound
Is really an impossible task
Grandma says "shush"
He says "can't they flush"
Is it really too much to ask?

Air conditioning is on
He's almost gone
Out of his very old mind
The wind it is blowing
And he sits there knowing
Each window is open he finds

Ten pop cans are open
He sits there mopin'
Barely is there gone a-sip
Against his own wishes
He's doing the dishes
You'd think they would leave him a tip.

Now all is quiet
There is no more riot
As his wife asks him to dance
With a wink and a smile

He hasn't seen in a while
He steps back and screams "not a chance."
Truth to be told
His wife is not old
She's the beauty that lives in each poem
But by the grace of God
He does fear the odds
At least grandkids eventually go home.

In high school I failed at football, the one thing I thought I was good at. I failed at algebra; something in my head just wouldn't click. (Ten years later in college I did get an A in algebra.) I had a shot at glory when I entered the Bayport wrestling invitational. I was seeded last with a record of two wins and two losses. There were three undefeated wrestlers there. I pinned the first two, which shocked my coaches. I called home; I was accomplishing something! Mom showed up drunk and screamed her terrible screams that reminded me of that night not so long ago. I was pinned in the championship bout and I cried. Not because I had lost, but because I felt humiliated hearing my Mother scream like that. I didn't lose because of the screaming; I lost because the other kid was a better wrestler than I was. I cried because of pride. I felt shame for who I was.

Despair

I wrote a sonnet
    A poem
    A verse
To the trees
To the sky

To the universe
That told of things
That never were
Told of dreams
That within me stir
To fly above the clouds
One day
To build great bridges
To earn my pay
To climb a mountain
To swim the sea
I could do all these things
Except I'm me!

My struggles were with my Mom. Dad drank, but he kept quiet.
He lost himself in his work. I just lost myself.

Take My Face

Trace me no etchings
Of a world I'll never see
Where waist-high grasses
Beckon to me with each step
The cackle of a rooster
Pheasant racing skyward
Partridge roosting
On the rooftops

Sell me no tickets
For unwritten plays
Deer and buffalo offering

Their lives for my life
A blanket to shed the cold

My eyes cry out
Take my face
Cup it in your hands
Hold me to your breast
Like you hold the bottle
That pierces your heart
Till the lies spill out
Like blood
On a freshly fallen snow.

I still feared coming home. I never knew what I was going to find. I feared sleeping, afraid of what I would wake to. I feared tomorrow, I feared yesterday; all I had to hold onto was today, this moment, right now. Nightmares.

Me Alone

Wooden stairs, varnished rails
Face pressed against oak bars
Poppa in boxer shorts, T-shirt
Sleeps a beer-induced sleep
On a couch that was a showpiece
For our place in society.

Momma in her bed torn
Calls me from the steps
Dreams out loud
Infecting the infection
With lead
Staining the couch

Their union paid for
In wasted dues.

I—a child
Could never sleep
Dreams dreamt
again and again
On other nights
With my face to the bars
Plays on in my orphanage
Where I run to me
And me alone.

I had nothing. I watched my sister die of brain cancer and my Dad speculate about whether part of the cause was marijuana. He suspected she smoked in college. I watched her die a long and hurtful death. I stayed away from drugs because I didn't want to go that way. Yet a fear that I'd die young haunted me.

I came home one Saturday night and found Mom passed out in bed. Nothing had been done all day. The next morning, I found her crawling to the bathroom and back to the bedroom. And the unsympathetic bastard that I was at the time hearkened back to the time I called the police on her. Yes, she needed help, but she learned far more destructive things while locked away. I had no one to give me guidance, no one I trusted; I was my own father, and a poor one at that.

I backed the car up to the front door and carried her out. Which wasn't easy because I weighed about 130 pounds and she weighed more than that, all dead weight. I drove her to St. Mary's Hospital, walked into the emergency room, and said "something's wrong with my Mother."

They took her in and I, like Pontius Pilate, washed my hands
of her.

Every Day

I ran into a mountain
Every day, every day
I ran into a mountain
I didn't know what to say
I ran into a mountain
Struggled with my truth
I ran into a mountain
There I lost my youth.

Babies love their Mommas
Mommas do the same
But love alone isn't strong enough
To win this human game
Brandy washed away her shame
Vodka drenched her soul
Secrets that she deemed to share
Which little boys shouldn't know
Crying in the orchard
Asking reasons why
A child lost inside herself
And Momma hoped to die.

And die she did
Every day, every day
And die she did
I didn't know what to say
And die she did

Struggling with my truth
And die she did
There I lost my youth.

Lies turn into stories
Stories cause great pain
Nobility spilled upon the floor
Drowned in poisoned rain
She struggled to hold onto life
Though a blood clot found its way
I found her there upon the ground
Another drunken day
Disgusted I packed up the car
Then hauled her into town
Like Pontius Pilate I washed my hands
A curse I can't live down.

A curse upon my shoulders
Every day, every day
A curse upon my shoulders
I didn't know what to say
A curse upon my shoulders
Struggling with my truth
A curse upon my shoulders
There I lost my youth.

Ghosts forever haunting
For my misguided thoughts
Was I thinking only of me
And all the wars I fought
It makes sense the things I did
When reasoned inside the head

But one unguarded moment
Could have left my Momma dead.

Every day, every day
I don't know what to say
Struggling with my truth
Facing a painful youth.

On November 8, the phone call came. I was called out of class (I still hate phone calls), and my Dad said, "If they don't operate on Mom right away, she'll die. Meet me at St. Vincent's Hospital."

St. Vincent's, that's where I'd watched my sister die.

Three times during those months, Dad called and said I had to get to the hospital right away because Mom wasn't going to make it. The blood clot on her brain was winning, even though it had been removed. I didn't do a lot of praying this time; I had learned you can't make deals with God. This time when the world got too heavy, I just ran. I'd run and run and run some more until I couldn't run anymore. Then I shook it off, lit a cigarette, and walked back to the hospital. A curious thing: cafeteria food, I didn't really sweat. Isn't that something?

I Don't Know

On the lonely side of eighteen
Running hard and running fast
Trying to catch my future
Trying to lose my past
If stupid were a teacher
I'd be first in my class
I don't know, I don't know

The stories I've been given
Handed down throughout the years
Depression in the bottle
Sugar in the tears
I'm all alone on Monday
And feel I have no peers
I don't know, I don't know

As the eagle flies to heaven
With my only prayer
Crowds stand on the sidewalk
Gathered just to stare
And people of position
Say they just don't care
I don't know, I just don't know.

I went to church with my Dad. When you're tracking a deer and you lose the track, you always go back to the point where you knew where you were, the last track. Going to church always seems like a very Polish/Catholic/Indian way to face life. The point at which you know where you are.

Choir Boy

It was a once in a lifetime thing
Standing in church at Dad's right arm
Where I should be, carrying his name
A gift generations in the making
The organ peeled away the roof
And for the very first time
"God Bless America"

Rang toward the sky
My Father's broken graveled voice
Groaned the notes with love
With respect and I—
Immature to a point—smiled
Caught a dirty look
We never spoke of the moment
My Father sang
But I'm sure
The angels in heaven
Joined the anthem
And God smiled.

Sitting in the hospital for three months gives a person a lot of time to think.

Thinking

There's a lot to be said for thinking
Reflecting on our days
Pondering every high and low
The ins and outs upon our way
Greeting the sun in the morning
Kissing the moon at night
There's a lot to be said for thinking
And I think that it's alright.

By the grace of God, Mom survived.

IV.

In June 1973, I was helping the neighbors move a garage my Father had purchased. It was a big garage, twenty-four feet by thirty feet. I went up to get gasoline for the car at the Oneida gas station, and Mr. Coonen came out and offered me a job. "Work as many hours as you want," he said. The same day I was also offered a job moving houses. I took the gas station job and ended up working forty-five hours a week all during my senior year. Our school promoted the concept of "cooperate and graduate," so I cooperated and graduated with a 1.787 grade point average.

On June 2, 1974, the announcement at school said that Shade Information Systems, a computer paper printing company, was taking applications. I went over, along with one of my white friends. This was the time of great affirmative action programs. My friend was hired as a $2.82 per hour materials handler. I was hired as a janitor.

Oh, well, I made a good janitor. A very lucky janitor, because the head of my department disagreed with the Human Resources director and said that anyone who worked for him deserved $3.32 an hour. Later, I learned I had started out making 50 cents an hour more than even the newly hired press operators. Within two weeks I was promoted to materials handler second shift.

It was a busy summer. We worked twelve-hour shifts through the week and usually sixteen-hour shifts on Fridays. We were putting out tons of product. My operators, Bob, Bob, and Scotty, were very pleased with my work. I took care of presses 7, 8, and 9. As the summer went on, my lead man also assigned me press 6, and I had to run down to press 2 and unload boxes. I was running around frazzled, but it was non-union work, and we were making lots of money. I also had to get my own materials with the forklift and haul away the finished product.

At the end of the summer, everyone got big raises. Everyone except me. My operators were quite upset and urged me to talk to the supervisor. I was nervous because I had always believed that if you kept your mouth shut and worked hard, then the rewards would come your way. But finally I did ask my supervisor why I didn't get a raise. He said it was apparent I was having trouble keeping up. I asked if he knew what I did. Naturally, he said he knew my duties, that I was to take care of presses 8 and 9. I suggested we take a walk, and I showed him what I did. He said he'd give it some thought. My operators, Bob and Scotty from 8 and 9, were called into the office.

The next day I received a 29-cent raise, was assigned only presses 8 and 9, and no longer had to get my own materials or haul away the finished product. Seems I had been doing quite a bit of the lead man and assistant lead man's work.

The company had a newspaper called *Shade Ink*, and at Christmas time they had a story contest. I won and was subsequently offered a part-time writing job for the paper; they paid me time and one-half for my duties. I was paid quite well, actually.

I received a promotion, and after training to run press 2, I set a production record on my first night as operator. My new supervisor, the old press 2 operator, didn't believe it. He held the previous record, which had been 800,000 business forms in an eight-hour shift. My first night, I produced 880,000 forms. The 100 percent goal each night was 640,000 forms. He singlehandedly counted and recounted my production record. Within three months, the 100 percent goal was raised to 800,000 forms in an eight-hour period.

Around this time, I wanted to get married.

I was eighteen, Debbie was eighteen, and we were in love. I was working two to three jobs and we had money, so why not get married? She was my best friend. Debbie's parents said no, but we were both of legal age. I wanted to get married in the church. I might not have been a good Catholic, but I was still a Catholic, and we are supposed to be a forgiving bunch.

The priest said we were too young. I said we were going to get married and it was up to the priest whether we got married in the church. We were married on February 14, 1975, in St. Norbert Chapel on the St. Norbert College campus. Eleven months later we started a family, and Dr. Seuss and I became good friends.

As our union blossomed, my beautiful wife, Debbie, urged me to go to college.

Rainbow Woman

Here you are safe
She said without words
As pain fell from my eyes
Rolling like thunder
'Cross the purple horizon
Sobs muffled in a pillow

Here you are safe
Her hands said
Caressing gently
My head
My heart
These are not tears
These are not tears
Mumbling in humiliation
Indians don't cry

Here you are safe
Her breath
Soft upon my neck
In silence a blessing
Our breath united
Calm like a mirrored lake

Here I am safe
In the spirit
In the love
Promised in youth
Held through the years.

We were living "high on the hog," but it really wasn't the type of life we envisioned for our family. We just wanted something better. We had plenty of money, we went out Saturday nights, we had friends, but we wanted more.

We read *Black Elk Speaks*, and we started to think differently.

Tradition

No tobacco
No beer
Branded by stereotypes
Johnny Cash, Ira Hayes
An idol, a hero
Punished for living
A healthy lifestyle
For far too long.

No tobacco
No beer

Allowed first in line
Soup kitchens, Councils
Broccoli, decaf
Skim milk
Point of Order.

No tobacco
No beer
Do they even know me?
My name?
My history?
Do they care?

No tobacco
No beer
No respect
No tradition.

Debbie and I attempted to see what we wanted our life to be like in the future, for ourselves and for our children, not knowing how many that would be. We really did find our interest piqued when we read about the Indian way of life, our traditions that were slowly disappearing. I also looked deeply at the people whom I admired and their ways of life.

Naturally, the people I first looked up to in this life were those who surrounded our families. My family was surrounded by hardworking journeymen. These men were all craftsmen in painting, carpentry, or cement work. Hardworking, hard-drinking men who hunted and played cards and took a stand for the United States of America and all that she stood for.

My Dad was a painter and wallpaper hanger, first and foremost. One of his proudest moments that I witnessed occurred around 1966 when he purchased a Plymouth Belvedere station wagon. The car itself wasn't what he was proud of; rather, it was the freedom that the car allowed him. Now he was able to transport his own tools from job to job, which helped him to increase his income. The first thing he bought was a wallpapering table (which I still own and use from time to time).

We worked all of the time. For as long as I can remember. Dad would say, "I can work a couple of hours and buy more fish than all those people fishing." So we worked. The only hobby we really had was hunting, and this was done more as a traditional type of thing. The knowledge and experiences were shared with each generation.

Dad was a proud working man; but with Mom's drinking problem, when the opportunity to become a painter inside a factory opened up, my Dad took it for the security of the insurance and the retirement benefits. "That insurance saved my a——," he said after Mom got sick in 1972. Late at night, drinking beer, as the stories flowed, he always spoke of his respect for the well-educated man. "When you can call someone an SOB and have him walk away smiling, then you've got the world at your fingertips," he said.

I have to give great accolades to Debbie. We could have had a "normal," middle-class, Green Bay life. Working, buying a three-bedroom ranch, watching the Packers on Sunday, and attempting to lead a safe and happy lifestyle. Instead she stood by my side and said, "Let's chase dreams."

I wrote this poem for her.

Hope (Is Debbie)

She led me to the mountain
With a smile that spoke of Dawn

The temptress called tomorrow
My future coming on
To be all that we can be
The seventh-generation thing
Cuddled in her hands my heart
She gave my soul its wings

All my life I wandered
Attempting to fit in
Cursed by words and memories
The color of my skin
Through the blue horizon
The smoky barroom din
Crowded in the canopy
She kept my soul from sin
Accolades I pay
To the few and chosen elite
Hope gives way to dreams
Set on the road to meet.

We ran away from home. We left Green Bay, with two young children in tow, and we headed for Oshkosh so I could go to college. We had enough money, if we scrimped, for a year. We had no insurance, and we lived in a depressing apartment with crooked floors, but Debbie made it our home.

With any food we purchased, we focused on the children—milk being the priority. Meat vanished from the table, but Debbie, like my Grandmother, became a potato magician. Yes, we both worked whenever work was available. And on some special Friday nights we would get a ninety-nine-cent bottle of wine and share a pizza. And in my spare time, I wrote.

I—A Poet

I
I am a poet
I manufacture dreams
Sending them
Wrapped in
Cellophane prayers
To the heavens
Fire, smoke
Circling in the sky

I
I am a poet
Exposing sins, shadows
Hidden in the crevasses
Of one's mind
Cascading down
Polluted waterfalls
Emerging as tainted foam
Floating out to sea

I
I am a poet
Enduring the taste
Of humility, ridicule
By the deaf and blind
Seeking shelter from the storm
We call life
While I
Dance in the rain
I am a poet.

Debbie and I couldn't afford for both of us to attend school, so I brought home everything I could and shared it with her. We were introduced to many good and great writers. I had to attend talks and plays for class assignments, and one night there was both a speaker and a play I was supposed to write papers about. I attended the lecture, and Debbie saw the play, *Godspell*. We soon became hooked on musicals. *Camelot*, *Jesus Christ Superstar*, and *Man of La Mancha* became staples in our home.

We returned to Green Bay for Thanksgiving. Wednesday evening, Mom had a kettle of pea soup cooking on the stove. Debbie loved pea soup, though I could only think of the *Exorcist* movie. But there was meat in the soup, so I nibbled it. The soup was terrific. I grew up a little bit that night.

Our oldest child was ready for kindergarten. The closest school was a Catholic school, near enough that we could walk with him back and forth every day. We arranged my classes so I could pick him up after school. We gave it a lot of thought. I remembered being the only Indian in a Catholic school.

Red/White

A solitary milk carton
White
With the letters
H-O-M-O-G-E-N-I-Z-E-D
Splayed red
Across the side

Perched atop
A plastic pail
Like an afterthought

With others of the same
Only different
Cartons of chocolate milk
Woven together in nuance

The procession begins
11:55 a.m.
Each and every day
Carried by the chosen
Anointed as knights
By well-meaning icons
Dressed in Black and White
Bent on saving
Heathen souls
My soul

A solitary milk carton
The same yet different
Always different
For the lack of a penny
A penny each day
I prayed
Counting three pennies
In my pocket
For an extra chocolate carton
Held ransom
For three pennies
I could be the same
Almost
A single white milk carton
In a sea of brown

A single little Indian
In the Catholic school
Downtown.

I went to Catholic school for eight years; I knew about religious traditions. Genuflecting on the right knee, making the sign of the cross with the right hand, praying the rosary, foundations for life—tradition. I saw *Fiddler on the Roof*, which is all about tradition. And I started thinking, why do these people, Catholics and Jews, survive when they could very well have been wiped out over the centuries? I started thinking, why are my people, the Indians, not surviving? I came to the conclusion that in order for a people to survive, their traditions must survive. The first thing the invaders from Europe did to the Indians was to take away their traditions and their voices. Traditions are important; traditions lay the foundations from which we can fly. Debbie and I made a decision. We would become fully participating Catholics. We would grab onto tradition. We would send our oldest child to Catholic school—but we would buy him chocolate milk.

Church has changed quite a bit since Vatican II as we've become more liberal. I remember watching all of my hardworking cousins and many hardworking farmers in our community, Oneida, crammed into the last pews of the church like sardines in a can on Sunday morning. It seemed that before Vatican II, no one ever missed mass.

Church

There is nothing quite as comfortable
As a wooden pew in church
Or so it seems

For when I dream
It's there that I am perched

Through no disguise
I close my eyes
And really try to pray
I do not choose
To begin to snooze
During sermons on Sunday

My wifey smiles
But after a while
If I begin to snore
I understand
The touch of her hand
I know what it is for.

We kept having babies, as good Catholics do. I realized I had to
get a real job and would have to go to night school to finish my
degree. I applied and was hired as assistant building supervisor
at the Winnebago County Courthouse. A week later, the Human
Resources Department called me into the office and told me that
I couldn't be the assistant building supervisor, after all. Instead,
they would give me the same pay and the same duties, but they
were going to call me a maintenance worker. I didn't understand,
but what could I do? Some people said "maintenance worker"
meant "janitor" but with more responsibilities. At least I received
higher pay. In the long run, I didn't receive the benefits the man-
agement position would have paid. Curious.

My in-laws, Gene and Lue, offered to help us with a down
payment, and we purchased a little two-bedroom house in the

city of Omro. We now had four children and lived like the Ingalls family in *Little House on the Prairie*. I cut a hole in the living room ceiling and made a bedroom in the attic. We joined the St. Mary's congregation and started teaching catechism. Then we started coaching Little League baseball. We had a lot of stuff; the only thing we lacked was money. Thankfully, a turkey farm in Chilton sold turkey meat quite inexpensively. At thirty pounds for $7.50, we always purchased sixty pounds, which amounted to about sixty-four drumsticks. Debbie became a turkey magician. We ate so much turkey that I developed a double chin, but when I started developing pin feathers instead of whiskers we cut back.

Life away from home at times seemed like a card game; I always held the hope that the next card would produce a better life. I became a gambler.

Gambling

Trying to stretch a dollar
Watch the fuel gauge light come on
Only two more miles down the road
And I pray to make it home

I turned into a gambling man
I gamble everyday
Working hard to make ends meet
Till the eagle lands I pray
I gambled that my car would make it
As I'm walking in the rain
With a can full of gasoline
Back to the car again.

One time, our Human Resources director decided to teach us a lesson. The courthouse workers association hadn't signed its latest contract in time. So the director withheld the full amount of our insurance payment from our checks until the contract was signed. Our paycheck withholding was two weeks in advance of the new month, and unfortunately for me, it was two weeks before the new year, just before Christmas. I lost a third of my paycheck. Everyone said not to worry, that I would be reimbursed after the new year. It hurt people like me who lived paycheck to paycheck. I couldn't put off Christmas.

Biblical Questions

Who is this god you give your money to
Banished from your government
Banished from your schools
His symbols on your money
Like Indians we've been told
How you honor god
Your actions leave me cold.

Genesis 1 thru 1492
Living on Turtle Island
Doing what men are called to do
Learning, laughing, crying
Sinning, stumbling, dying.

Exodus since 1492
Forced into bondage
As animals are forced to do
Herded, driven, bred
Culled and killed

now dead.
But honored
As a mascot.

I knew the actions weren't directed toward me alone, but that they really hurt all the lowest-paid people at the courthouse, most notably the minority population who worked there. Why would a government purposely hurt people?

Same Old, Same Old

He smiled at us and said
My Great Grandmother was
An Indian Princess
Born and bred
Within the boundaries
Of the great Cherokee Nation
I love the Indian ways
Fry Bread and Pow Wows
Jingle Dancers and Casinos
Then he walked away
Taking his smile
My wife looked at me
Said: "You look skeptical."
I replied,
"I have reservations."

Often I was recognized as an Indian, maybe more often than I noticed. People would engage me in conversation, pouring out their admiration for "my People" and sharing their stories about ancestors being of our blood.

I went to night school, and in the academic field I did quite well. I was graded and respected for my work. So, more and more I believed Debbie and I had made the right decision in running away from our old life and focusing on building a better life for our family through education.

There was a chance for a promotion at work. Assistant building supervisor, wouldn't you know. My boss told me I had the best interview. Naturally, they hired someone else. It just so happened there were two projects that needed doing. Both projects required carpentry skills, and my new boss, the assistant building supervisor, was a carpenter.

I was assigned to the first project: building a television and VCR bookcase for the "Help Line/Suicide Help Line Center." For the second project, my boss had to frame in a four-by-five-foot window and panel the sides, creating an opening that could be opened and closed during business hours. I built mine on Monday, varnished it on Tuesday, and delivered it on Wednesday. By the end of the week, my boss's project still wasn't finished. They fired him the following Monday morning.

That same day, the night supervisor at the courthouse came and congratulated me, telling me that I had received the position. WRONG! I asked why. I was told the man they hired instead had his own tools. What kind of answer was that?

Circles

History repeats itself
There's lessons to be learned
About what really happened
Before the page was turned
Aesop was a dwarf some say

Who liked to tell tall tales
If Isaac was a teenager
That story may have failed
David slew the GIANT
But was David a peeping Tom
Solomon in all his glory
Why is his kingdom gone
A Son was sent to show the way
We hung Him up on high
Now we have religious wars
It makes the spirits cry
Columbus sailed the ocean blue
Never seeking help along the way
Thought he landed in India
Just east of old Bombay
The natives welcomed Columbus and crew
Surely a sight to behold
Things haven't changed really too much
For Indians, or so I'm told.

Naturally, I was angry. Naturally, I was hurt. I couldn't understand.
I still don't. Still, I strove, and still strive, to be a man of honor. For,
at the end of the day, I have to look back and live with myself.

Bite My Tongue

One thing that I've come to learn
'Bout this Indian condition
It's not always about the cash
But it's always about position
I was always second rate

No matter what I achieved
Did my best—bit my tongue
Even loved ones didn't believe
I set records at the shop
And quality produced
They said you should do even more
So my raises were reduced
Then a prize before my eyes
I was hired as an assistant
One month later—to no surprise
The position became nonexistent
The job remained, the money too
But the title—it had vanished
I did my best, I bit my tongue
My dreams were all but banished
I won the races, overachieved
Whenever they gave a test
They were sorry, despite test scores
I was always second best.

Thank the Lord, I really have had a great life. A lot of people whom I've respected respected me. I was (am!) in love with my wife. We have great children. I coached Little League, and my wife was my dugout coach. The kids called her "Coach Honey."

It took a few years, but we finally got things right in my coaching program. At the end, thanks to a free substitution rule, we played all of our fifteen players the same number of innings per game. And everyone had to play every position at least once except for catcher, which was a position you only played if you wanted to. Each player had to pitch. We had a player who'd had a stroke as a child. He had limited use of one arm, and he had a weak leg. He played first base and pitched. We went undefeated two of those last six years, and we made a lot of memories.

In my final year of coaching, I helped coach a team of fourteen-year-olds, and we won the Oshkosh championship. I earned my greatest compliment from a Winneconne player who said to me, "No wonder you guys always win. They've got you as a coach."

Little League

The greatest words
I ever heard
Are:
"Balls in, comin' down."

Let church bells ring
For every spring
It's:
"Balls in, comin' down."

The triumph of men
To be boys again
"Balls in, comin' down."

Moms and Dads
The best times we've had
"Balls in, comin' down."

Win or lose today
Just let us play
"Balls in, comin' down."

The greatest words
I ever heard
Are:
"Balls in, comin' down."

I taught religion. I was on the church board. I wrote. I was happy.

I contemplated the universe and heaven! Then one day I listened to a group of people discussing the things their parents would scold them about, so I wrote:

Heaven's Gate

I was standing in line at heaven's gate
Feeling quite anxious, I really couldn't wait
To see St. Peter so old, so wise
Would he let me into this paradise?

My apprehensions were growing stronger
As the reject line was getting longer
All these poor souls a fussin' and cryin'
A murmur from some "your Momma weren't lyin'."

One sad reject was heard to retort
Momma always said my skirt was too short
Another fell down on the ground on his knees
St. Peter simply said, "You didn't eat your peas."
Meant to eat all of my food, said another poor soul
Those starving in Africa, how did Momma know
I thought it was just something Mothers said
Who knew I'd be judged now that I'm dead
Another fair lady her brow all crinkled

Momma said don't wear clothes that are wrinkled
Now I'm rejected, ejected, and gone
Momma always said these things were wrong.

But me I wasn't worried
As alone I stood there
Before my fatal accident
I put on clean underwear.

V.

They say each man's home is his castle. It really was true, as I lived within my home, within the walls of my family. Only when I ventured outside of my castle walls did I encounter obstacles. Otherwise I lived within a halo of rainbows and lollipops. Actually, sloppy joes and potato chips (my traditional birthday meal).

Daydreaming

Once upon a star so high
Butterflies floated down from the sky
Turning to snowflakes as they fell
Landing on eyelashes so I could tell
That rainbows racing across my view
Brought joy to all the folks I knew
Dancing along the world at bay
Making tomorrow's all today
Once upon a star so high
I saw heaven in the sky.

Debbie and I kind of conceded we could have money or we could have kids. We chose kids. Our lives were engulfed by kids and their interests. Louie, Jacob, Jordan, and Philip all played baseball. Our girls had their own interests. Dawn was into gymnastics until we ran out of money, and yet it lives with her still. Renee was into everything.

This poem, "Job Jar" (selected for the Wisconsin Fellowship of Poets' 2018 Calendar), sums up our beliefs on raising kids.

Job Jar

I meant to clean the car today
Erase the "wash me" tattoos

Destroy evidence of
Birds' bombing raids
Scrub bugs' last acts
From the windshield
I meant to clean the car today
My wife's leftover popcorn
From the five-dollar cinema
Sunflower seed shells
From a would-be ball player
Tissues tucked helter-skelter
Hidden with lipstick, nail polish
I meant to clean the car today
The tic-tac-toe
On the dust-covered dash
Finger-painted windows
Root beer stains and mud
I meant to clean the car today
But my son said, "Hey Dad
Do you want to play catch
Hit a few
Catch a few
Pretend a bit?"
I meant to clean the car today
Oh well!

Then, as the children grew and went away to school, I would sometimes be sent on "care package" deliveries, often having first to stop at the store. On one such delivery run, while stopping at a new supermarket, I encountered some banking people who were attempting to earn their living.

Pi R Squared

I went down to the grocery store to get some peanut butter
For my child away at school with instructions from their
mudder
In a strange store east of I don't know, I felt so all alone
I stuck out like a sore thumb so far away from home
When a strange lady grabbed my arm and pulled me to
her side
"Do you think you're smarter than a fifth grader?" "Well,
of course I am," I lied.
A fifth grader would have yelled like hell when approached
by someone strange
All I did was shake my head and agree to play her game
Spin the wheel she smiled at me and so that's what I did
Around and around and around and around stopping at a
question for a first-grade kid
The question was easy I did just fine getting a math test
right
The second-grade question came to me, "p.m." means that
it's night
The third-grade question came and went, the fourth-grade
question too
Then the final question a fifth-grade one, what was I to do?
If I'm right I win a chance to go to a Packer game
Or a chance to star on television with Aaron Rodgers's name
They wanted the symbol for pi r squared I knew they were
going down
Everyone knows that pie aren't square
Pie are really round!

I came to a point in my working life when I knew I wasn't going to advance. Then I saw an ad for a job opening at the highway department; they needed a janitor. Hey, hey, hey, a job right up my alley. No, I didn't want to be a janitor, but it was the starting position at the highway department. I applied, and I was turned down. Three, four, maybe even five times I was turned down for a janitor's job. I couldn't understand it. But because I couldn't advance where I was, I wanted to join a union where being an Indian didn't matter. So, I went to Human Resources, which began a vicious cycle of carrots being snatched from in front of this donkey's nose. They told me that because of my current job description, I wasn't qualified to be a janitor, but not to quit trying because "you gave a great interview." Talk about humiliation.

Janitor Blues

Bury my heart at Wounded Knee
Let me be what I wanna be
I don't live in no Tee Pee
All I have is a bachelor degree
Working nights
Singing the janitor blues.

I was told that I should see
Folks whose job is equality
Sitting there—committee
Affirmative action for you and me
Working nights,
Singing the janitor blues.

They said that you're a rising star
With your talent you'll go far
Riding in a big fine car

Driving the Man from bar to bar
Working nights
Singing the janitor blues.

In my interview I got
Explained a six-hundred-page manual on the spot
A snide old grin likely as not
My competition said, I quote, "I use it a lot."
Working nights
Singing the janitor blues.

I enjoyed it when they gave a test
I could prove that I was really the best
They went and hired one of the rest
Said people with feathers should stay on the nest
Working nights
Singing the janitor blues.

For years I was told, despite cum laude grade point averages
As I sought my degree, that I wasn't qualified to be a janitor.
Finally lies succumbed to the fires of truth only to be reborn,
As a Phoenix, to keep us in our place. Lies are weapons that
Can defeat the flesh but can never defeat our honor!

One day a urinal on the third floor of the courthouse backed up,
and water ran down the concrete walls between the floors until
it decided to drip on the Human Resources assistant director's
desk. Just deserts, wouldn't you say? It was clean water, but still
the thought was evilly enticing. I had to do quite a bit of plumbing
work on that project, and the little angel on my right shoulder was
having a fight with the little devil on my left shoulder—should I
tell her that the water was from the urinal?

Anyway, as I had to secure her ceiling, a false ceiling, she left for the day. Now, each time I had asked about the janitor's position, I was told that my current job description didn't qualify me for the new position. Apparently, Human Resources assumed I was a real idiot. Offhandedly, I asked the assistant director's secretary if I could possibly see my job description. After about ten minutes, she came back and said that there wasn't a job description for my position. This was probably from when I was hired for the assistant building supervisor job but then had the title taken away.

We had an affirmative action committee, so I attended a meeting and asked why I couldn't get a janitor's position with the county highway department. The HR person, who oversaw hiring for the entire county, became quite agitated and said, "I told you that your job description doesn't qualify you to be a janitor at the highway!" I asked to see the job description.

Later, I was contacted by a woman from the University of Wisconsin–Oshkosh who encouraged me to contact the ACLU. Eventually I did, but my case didn't make the cut. One little Indian who couldn't get a promotion apparently didn't count. They only had so many funds.

I'm Alive

White men came to take away
Our hopes,
Our dreams,
Our yesterdays,
Give up what is yours, we'll make it mine
Just sign right here on the dotted line
Then stand aside . . . beyond the door
We don't want to hear your voice no more

It's not your hair
It's not your car
It's not even you
It's what you are!

I'm alive

Branded 666 on the White man's cross
Christ the King is at a loss
How Christians turn
Deaf ear
Blind eye
To the wretched truth
That I'm alive.

I went to your schools I bought into your dream
Discovered that life ain't all it seems
In the comic books or on the movie screen
The lines of your writing should be read between
When through your actions you say I'm sub-par
It's not you. . . . It's what you are!

I'm alive

So my family suffers for my birth
For the shade of my skin is what I'm worth
On the open market good people turn blind
They won't believe it happens in our time
It's not your hair
It's not your car
It's not even you
It's what you are.

I'm alive

Soooooooooooooooo, I applied for the janitor's position again. This time they said they were going to hire two people, but instead they decided to hire only one. "Sorry, Louie, but you were the second choice."

Soooooooooooooooo, I applied for the janitor's position again. This time they said they were going to hire two people, but instead they decided to hire only one. "Sorry, Louie, but you were the second choice."

Soooooooooooooooo, I applied for the janitor's position again. This time they said they were going to hire two people, but instead they decided to hire only one. "Sorry, Louie, but you were the second choice."

I'm nothing if not persistent. Then it was, "They were going to hire three, Louie, but they hired only two, and you were the third choice. But if either one of them quits before their probation, you get the job!"

Denied Again

I played the game
But just the same
The rules can change
At any time

No sweet repose
For I never rose
All doors were closed
To that skin of mine

My dreams to foil
A fresh-lanced boil

A life of toil
Too weak to fight

No wise sage
To turn the page
I battle age
Though not contrite

I carry on
Till hope is gone
Our history's long
A Redskins plight

To rub salt into my wounds, we started to get our fuel for the vehicles at the courthouse from the highway department. It seemed, could be my imagination, but every time that I was turned down for a janitor's position, somehow I ended up going to the highway department for fuel. It was not one of my normally assigned duties.

Then one day (set in my imagination to the background music of Handel's *Hallelujah Chorus*) as I was fueling the vehicle, a county truck came racing up to the fuel pumps. The driver said, "You the Indian from the courthouse that's trying to get a job out here? The janitor they hired just walked out; he quit." The driver smiled at me and said, "My wife's an Indian." Then he drove away.

I raced back to the courthouse and right up to the HR office. I asked the HR person, who had turned me down so many times before, if it was true that I was the third choice and that if one of the other two quit that I'd get the job. She seemed quite agitated that I would keep asking her, but she said, "Yes, it was true." That's when I told her that one of them had just quit. It was a sight to behold.

She started coughing and hacking, little snot balls flew from her nose—it was beautiful. A month later I started my new job. A little less per hour, but I was guaranteed overtime and a forty-hour work week. Seven months later, after becoming a union member, I received a promotion to grader operator.

Still See Red

When blessings came
They came in silence
We held our breath
Seven generations of fear
Seven generations of pain
Visions through tears
Our children suckled
At rubber bosoms
Mother's milk conscripted
Stolen by congress
Eagles were poisoned
Hawks became businessmen
Raccoons joined the BIA
We drowned in battle
Sugar-coated dreams
We disappeared
Our blood, our skin
Faded
But white minds
Still see red
Still see red
Still see red.

I tried to fit in. Often I thought I had. I guess I was wrong.

August 21, 1990. Things move slowly in this world. I received notification of my promotion in May, and this was my first day out of the shop. I was no longer a janitor. My first job was grinding and caulking cracks on the bridge decks on a section of Highway 41 known as the Causeway. My foreman was Auggie, an ex-marine who had served in Vietnam. A number of times throughout the day he came to me and said, "Louie, you don't have to work that hard."

I was just happy to be working outside, actually doing something I was good at. At the courthouse I always had to grind the sidewalk cracks and caulk them, but we always did it in the fall when the weather was cold. The caulk we used was stiff, and I devised a warming bucket with a light bulb for heat to keep the caulk pliable. The caulk the bridge crew used was self-leveling and pretty much heaven for a caulking man. I could have done that job forever until my knees gave out.

After lunch, a different county truck pulled up with a different foreman behind the wheel. He called me over, and the first words out of his mouth were, "You think you're pretty smart, don't you." I knew things were just going to go downhill after that.

He proceeded to tell me it was terrible I had used the "Indian card" to get myself a job at the highway department. But that was all I was going to have—it didn't matter how much schooling I had, I was never going anywhere at the County. There were a lot of F-words concerning me and my race spewing from his mouth, and he made it clear that I was nothing.

Who could have believed that this could happen in 1990.

December 4, 1990. It was just after midnight, Tuesday morning, during what would end up being one of the worst snowstorms in Winnebago County history. My grader was parked next to Gary, a man I had come to admire for his professionalism. I asked him what I was doing wrong, as I didn't seem to be cleaning up the road very well at all. He asked what I was doing, and when I explained that the man who'd trained me said to do X and Y, Gary laughed and said, "Don't listen to that SOB."

I came to discover that there were certain men I could trust because they were professionals. Thank you, Gary, my grader mentor, and John, who stood up for me.

Things were great on the home front, however. We were leading a normal life. There were ups and downs, though a lot more ups than downs. Work was something I had to do to keep the family moving. I went to school at night when I could. Our children were doing well in their lives. I was offered a job for a road construction crew at twice the hourly rate as I was receiving. We had to weigh this very heavily. If I took the job, I'd be gone almost all summer.

Money wasn't what the Clark family was about. We turned down the job, and I remained a significant part of the family.

I got called into the office at work one time and was questioned about the Pope's Doctrine of Infallibility.

I had never heard of such a thing. Later I researched the doctrine and came to wonder what that had to do with running a grader.

The funny thing, through the absurdity of it all, is that because of the union I was able to learn different jobs and skill sets. I think I was a good worker because no one ever complained about my finished product. After, I believe, scoring the highest on the foreman's test three times in a row, they said they threw out the first test, but admitted I had the highest score on the next two. Thanks to the union, I became a foreman.

It's funny, but because of my persistence, eventually I was the highest paid hourly worker at the county highway department. This alone filled me with an honor that allowed me to hold on.

Even when I had to put up with reasoning like this. (The name of my partner is changed to fit the poem.)

Smarter Than a Fourth Grader

Sometimes our comprehension
Of what we know as true
Is lost when bosses direct us
Telling us what to do
It happened on a cloudy night
When snow fell down like rain
We were sent out to do our jobs
Plowing the roads again.

The storm was hard and howling
It was really hard to see
We knew the roads were dangerous
My partner Tim and me
We plowed and plowed and plowed and plowed
Then we plowed and plowed some more
The storm was bad we couldn't keep up
So they called us off the road
Prepare yourselves our bosses said
Fuel up, clean up, reload.

We prepared to sleep at the shop
Our cars had nowhere to roam
Yet one boss thought himself special
He said, "I should sleep at home."

So he marched himself up to me
I knew I couldn't win
He asked who was it who plowed his road
"If it's done," I said, "it's Tim."

Attempting to control his temper
He said to me, "Now, son.
I have only one question:
Who did it if it's not done?"

I didn't know what to do or say
To the question that he gave
It was like a fourth-grade test
Who's buried in Grant's grave?

These were men I was supposed to trust. These were leaders, men
who were supposed to be honorable.

Questions

Questions always come to me
Daytime nightmares constantly
Evil dark and moist and cold
Bends my shoulders as I grow old
How did I sin to injure the man?
To be upright is no rebel stand
To seek what's true, honest, and fair,
Didn't ask for much, only my share
I stood tall, did my best
I survived, passed every test
Yet to him, within his sight
I never could do anything right

Yet the man, so honest and good
The whole world knew just where he stood
A heart of gold they all told me
But they didn't see what I had to see
A man of conflict in his soul
Who fought his prejudice this I know
Though he fought he could never win
Just being born was my greatest sin
His prejudiced ways sealed my fate
Years later I still pay for his hate
My family, too, must cope with the man
We pay a price for his ignorant stand
Does he pay for his sins now that he's gone
The feelings I hold are hurtful and wrong
As a good Christian man I seek to live
But thoughts of my loss
It is hard to forgive.

Those are the struggles I face every day. Forgiveness. The pain and humiliation were difficult to bear. Still, it is my job to respect them as human beings and treat them as I wish to be treated. I put this all on my own shoulders.

If I don't forgive them, I only hurt me.

Epilogue

A Christmas Gift

I saw the face of God today
As he sat next to me in church
His toothless grin
As I held his hand
Our eyes met
When we said hello
The choir sang
Bells were ringing
We both turned next to pray
A little old man
In a tattered coat
I saw God's face today

A certain smell
Drifted through the air
All across the pew
So I smiled
For in my years
Jesus had his smell too
With shaking hands
Into his purse
He put something
On the plate
A human being so worn away
I saw God's face today

I clasped his hand
With hollowed eyes
He smiled into my soul
A hint of mint
As he walked away
A little old man
In a tattered coat
I saw God's face today!

The End
(The beginning?)

Acknowledgments

Thanks to Kathy, Kate, and Daniel, for seeing something.

Thanks to Carrie for holding my hand, as it were.

Thank you to my family, Debbie, Louie and Alissa, Dawn and Andy, Renee and Jeff, Jacob, Jordan and Hillary, and Philip, and the continuing seven generations, Faith, Danny, Julia, Eliza, Addison, Camryn, Mara, Hope, Morgan, Elenore, Harrison, Zoe, Noah, and Jack!

About the Author

Louis V. Clark III was born on the Oneida reservation in Wisconsin. Raised during the 1960s, Clark learned to stand up for what he thought was right, aided by the guiding hand of many influential people. He joined forces with his beautiful wife during their high school years, and they ran away to build their own life guided by the principle of "looking ahead seven generations." Now that his six children have graduated from college, Clark is focusing on his dream of sharing his experiences in the hopes of building a better world. Blessed with fourteen grandchildren, he leans on his baseball background and says, "Never go down looking." This is his third book.

The eagerly awaited follow-up to the breakout memoir *How to Be an Indian in the 21st Century*, winner of the Midwest Booksellers Choice Award

In *Rebel Poet: More Stories from a 21st Century Indian*, writer Louis Clark returns to the themes of family, community, loss, and the struggle to make a place in the world when your very identity is considered suspect. He examines the effects of his mother's alcoholism and his young sister's death, offers an intimate recounting of the discrimination he faced as an Indian on the job, and celebrates the hard-fought sense of home he and his wife have created. Seamlessly mixing poetry and prose, the bitter and the sweet, *Rebel Poet* is at turns darker and more hopeful than its predecessor.

I am a poet
I manufacture dreams
Sending them
Wrapped in
Cellophane prayers
To the heavens
Fire, smoke
Circling in the sky

LOUIS V. CLARK III was born and raised on the Oneida Indian reservation in Wisconsin. He is a member of the Iroquois Confederacy and the Bear clan.

Wisconsin Historical Society
P R E S S

ISBN 978-0-87020-929-1

51595

9 780870 209291